Ayia Paraskevi Figurines
in the University of Pennsylvania Museum

Ayia Paraskevi Figurines
in the University of Pennsylvania Museum

Vassos Karageorghis

and

Terence P. Brennan

Published by
The University Museum
University of Pennsylvania
Philadelphia
1999

Design, editing, production
Publications Department, University of Pennsylvania Museum

Cover Design:
Bagnell and Socha, Bala Cynwyd, PA

Cover Photograph:
H. Fred Schoch

Printing
Sun Printing House, Philadelphia, PA

Library of Congress Cataloging-in-Publication

Karageorghis, Vassos.
  Ayia Paraskevi figurines in the University of Pennsylvania Museum /
Vassos Karageorghis and Terence P. Brennan.
      p. cm.
  Includes bibliographical references.
  1. Ayia Paraskevi Site (Nicosia, Cyprus)–Catalogs. 2. Terra-cotta
figurines–Cyprus–Ayia Paraskevi Site–Catalogs. 3. Bronze
age–Cyprus–Ayia Paraskevi Site–Catalogs. 4. University of
Pennsylvania. University Museum–Catalogs. I. Brennan, Terence P. II.
University of Pennsylvania. University Museum. III. Title.
  DS54.95.N53 K39 1999
  016.939'37–dc21
                                                99-006965

Contents

List of Figures

Introduction

Max Ohnefalsch-Richter on Cyprus

The 1870s and 1880s witnessed considerable archaeological activity on Cyprus. Among the first excavations were those of Luigi Palma di Cesnola, whose collection of Cypriot antiquities left the island and was shipped to New York in 1876. By exporting the collection, Cesnola not only deprived Cyprus of some of its most precious treasures but also set a precedent that encouraged the Cypriots themselves to carry out clandestine excavations for profit, knowing that there was a lucrative market for Cypriot antiquities. Despite the efforts of local British authorities to discourage unauthorized excavations, stopping such activity was an impossible task. The police could exercise only limited control in the countryside, and local legislation enacted in a number of towns proved ineffective. To make matters worse, the people who encouraged and protected the looters—and subsequently profited from their spoils—were influential citizens, often members of the government, who were immune from prosecution.

These illegal sales were occurring at a time when the regulations governing authorized excavations permitted the excavator to keep one-third of his finds (which he could sell if he chose). Of the remaining artifacts, one-third would go to the Cyprus Museum and the rest would be the property of the owner of the land. The landowner was also permitted to put his portion on the open market and was invariably enthusiastic about the prospect of selling to the highest bidder—often the excavator himself.

It was in this milieu of unregulated excavation that Max Ohnefalsch-Richter arrived in 1878, immediately following the British occupation of the island. The ambitious young German had come with the intention of photographing points of interest, but soon developed a taste for antiquities that both satisfied his "scholarly" curiosity and provided him with the material means to prolong his stay on the island. He excavated "legally" on behalf of various individuals (civil servants, bankers, and others), who provided him with financial backing. In addition to providing for his basic needs, Ohnefalsch-Richter's benefactors, in keeping with the conventions of the time, authorized his retention of a personal collection of antiquities.

He stayed on Cyprus for twelve years, from 1878 to 1890. During that time he excavated extensively at a number of sites on the island, including Salamis, Soloi, Idalion, Tamassos, Kourion, Ayia Paraskevi, Amathus, and Marion. In addition to the artifacts he acquired as a fringe benefit of his role as excavator, he also purchased objects from tomb-looters. These latter acquisitions he eventually sold to museums abroad. (Many articles about Ohnefalsch-Richter's activities on Cyprus have appeared in recent years; for more information, please see the Bibliography at the end of this volume.)

Ohnefalsch-Richter had close relations with various foreign museums, mainly in Europe, but also in the United States. There was a great interest in Cypriot antiquities, a trend that had begun in America with the Metropolitan Museum of Art in New York. Beginning in 1890, he lectured in both Europe and the United States—primarily to discredit the work of Cesnola. Ohnefalsch-Richter considered himself a far more careful excavator, following the model of Heinrich Schliemann, whose work he admired and praised. It was during these lecture tours that he found the opportunity to sell antiquities to a number of museums. In addition to the University of Pennsylvania Museum in Philadelphia, other institutions known to have purchased antiquities from Ohnefalsch-Richter include the Johns Hopkins University museum in Baltimore, the Kunsthistorisches Museum in Vienna, and the Fitzwilliam Museum in Cambridge. He also sold pieces to museums in Berlin and Karlsruhe, and many of the antiquities that he found at Tamassos are now in the Royal Ontario Museum.

One hundred years have elapsed since the discovery of the figurines discussed here, yet Max Ohnefalsch-Richter remains one of the early "romantic" figures in Cypriot archaeology. In contrast to Cesnola, he possessed a "scholarly" curiosity and made efforts to publish his discoveries. To his credit, even at this early stage in development of the science of archaeology, he had the vision to present the ancient culture of Cyprus within its Mediterranean context. His *magnum opus, Kypros, the Bible and Homer* (1893), betrays vast erudition, although his views, mainly about art and religion, betray arbitrary generalizations and do not fulfill the requirements of modern scholarship.

As a scholar, he must have been respected by the then young Oxford archaeologist John L. Myres, with whom he collaborated on the publication in 1899 of *A Catalogue of the Cyprus Museum*. But, unlike Myres whose interests were purely scholarly and who proved to be a sound scholar in the true sense of the word, Ohnefalsch-Richter did not avoid some of the "sins" committed earlier by Cesnola. He unscrupulously bought ancient objects from local tomb-looters and considered antiquities to be merchandise that could be traded for personal profit. In a letter to the German archaeologist Adolf Furtwängler, he admitted that he sold the contents of one tomb that he excavated at Tamassos in order to pay for medical treatment when his wife was ill. On the other hand, it was primarily through his influence that Prime Minister Gladstone established a museum in Nicosia, which became the well-known Cyprus Museum.

Although the rise of Cypriot archaeology as a well-respected field incorporating the highest standards of research was probably the result of the work done by Myres as well as the later efforts of the Swedish Cyprus Expedition (1929–1932), the phenomenon of Max Ohnefalsch-Richter was, in some ways, an inevitable step in this process of development.

The Acquisition of the Collection

The seventeen objects described below represent only a small portion of the Cypriot antiquities in the collections of the University of Pennsylvania Museum of Archaeology and Anthropology that were purchased in the early 1890s from Max Ohnefalsch-Richter. The objects discussed here were found at Nicosia-Ayia Paraskevi, either by Ohnefalsch-Richter in his excavations, or by tomb-looters, from whom he purchased the objects. He described and illustrated most of the pieces in his publication, *Kypros, the Bible and Homer* (1893: 427, pl. LXXXVI). Although eschewed by scholarly museums these days, the practice of acquiring archaeological artifacts by purchase was normal and legal at the time and did occur frequently in the early years of this museum. It was often a means of supplementing the collections that had been amassed through excavation.

Established in 1887 by a group of prominent Philadelphians, The Museum of Archaeology and Palaeontology, as the museum was originally called, had as its founding mission the scientific exploration of human cultures, both past and present, and the dissemination of the resulting knowledge to the public. Central to this mission was the fairly novel notion that the museum should send out its own representatives to conduct fieldwork on its own behalf and gather not only artifacts but also the all-important associated data. In 1889 the museum embarked on its first large-scale archaeological expedition abroad, excavating at the site of Nippur in modern-day Iraq, and within a decade had several projects underway around the world simultaneously.

As its collections grew and its reputation spread, support for the museum and interest in its activities increased. In 1889, the museum moved to a more spacious building and first opened its doors to the public. Before 1895, ambitious plans were underway to construct an even larger building for the purpose of housing its present and future collections and providing increased space for exhibitions.

Having become increasingly aware of its role as an educational resource in the community, the museum recognized the need, on the one hand, to present to the public the history of material culture in a more comprehensive and unified fashion, and, on the other, to expose young scholars in training at the University of Pennsylvania to a broader sample of artifacts. Accordingly, the museum began to purchase artifacts in order to fill certain chronological and geographical gaps in the collection and to serve as study collections and representative samples.

Sara Yorke Stevenson, a founder of the museum and one of its most tireless supporters, was among those on the staff who consistently augmented the collections in this fashion, obtaining through purchase select specimens of types of objects that it would have been otherwise impossible or impractical to acquire. First as curator of the Egyptian Section and later as curator of the newly established Mediterranean Section, Stevenson was responsible for a prolonged period of acquisition in this manner that, for a time, earned the museum a reputation as being most eager to acquire antiquities from legitimate scholars.

Such activity brought the museum, and Sara Yorke Stevenson in particular, to the attention of Max Ohnefalsch-Richter. At his instigation, they began a correspondence which lasted nearly ten years. In his letters, housed in the University of Pennsylvania Museum Archives, Ohnefalsch-Richter treats Stevenson sometimes as his confidante, advocate, mentor, and patron, but always as a potential buyer of his antiquities.

Lamenting his persistent lack of funds, Ohnefalsch-Richter at times entreats her to obtain money for him to excavate on behalf of the museum, implores her to gather subscriptions to underwrite the cost of publishing his work, or urges her to arrange his lecture tours in the United States. Nearly every letter includes a sales pitch in which Ohnefalsch-Richter proffers Stevenson antiquities from his collection for sale, or offers his services on commission to act as an agent for the museum in acquiring certain Cypriot artifacts. As far as can be ascertained from the existing documentation in the University of Pennsylvania Museum archives, Stevenson never arranged funds for Ohnefalsch-Richter to excavate under the auspices of the museum on Cyprus nor did she accept his offer to serve as an agent of the museum for the purposes of securing Cypriot antiquities. She did, however, purchase two separate lots of objects from him, the second lot consisting only of a single hermaphroditic statue.

It is the first lot that concerns us here and of which the objects described below formed a part. In a letter offering these objects for sale, Ohnefalsch-Richter introduced the material in this way:

> A most interesting collection of antiquities and ethnographical articles is herewith offered to you. I have collected it myself in the island of Cyprus during a stay of 12 years. But this, what I have to offer, does not consist in big or beautiful pieces of sculpture, gold-ornaments, etc. This little collection is notwithstanding of great scientific value and perhaps even of a much higher value from the scientific standpoint, than the collections of much higher market and money value.

In November of 1892, evidently in response to a request from Stevenson for further information, Ohnefalsch-Richter sent a catalogue describing and illustrating the objects he was offering for sale to the museum, 304 in all—204 ancient objects and 100 ethnographic objects included for the purposes of comparison because he thought them to be illustrative of survivals of ancient customs. From this catalogue Stevenson compiled one of her own, taking excerpts from some entries, apparently summarizing others, and including Ohnefalsch-Richter's illustrations of certain objects.

Stevenson's catalogue and the resulting ledger book that was produced from it are virtually the only documents in the University of Pennsylvania Museum archives that shed light on the earliest descriptions and reputed proveniences and sources of the antiquities purchased by the museum from Ohnefalsch-Richter. Having said as much, though, the information contained in these documents regarding those important details is lamentably deficient, particularly with respect to the objects that form the subject of the present study. The most informative of the entries concerns MS 69-74: "All these objects . . . are from the Nekropolis of Hagia Paraskevi. Dr. Richter bought them from secret excavators, but they are identical with the objects exhumed by himself." The remainder of the objects described below, MS 75-81, 84, 85, 91, and 488, are merely noted as having come from the necropolis at Ayia Paraskevi with no indication given as to whether they were excavated by Ohnefalsch-Richter himself or were bought from tomb-looters.

Following their purchase, all 304 objects were accessioned into the collection of the Mediterranean Section and, as they were the first objects to be acquired by that newly created department, received the first identification numbers issued by the section and were placed on exhibition. The ethnographic objects were subsequently de-accessioned and sold at auction in 1949. The remaining artifacts, having previously been removed from display, were evidently sorted by artifact type and ware, placed into trays, and housed in a corridor in the Mediterranean Section.

As sometimes happens in large museums, one tray became separated from the others and was inexplicably mislaid. The existence and exact location of the artifacts contained therein, those described below, thus remained effectively concealed from the scholarly world until a fortuitous set of events brought them to light again. In the Fall of 1994, during a three-year-long renovation of the museum's Cypriot storerooms, numerous artifacts were rediscovered, including the objects in the aforementioned tray. At that time Dr. Karageorghis was visiting the museum in order to examine several other pieces in the Ohnefalsch-Richter collection and, recognizing the objects that were thought by the scholarly world to have been lost, brought them to the attention of the staff of the Mediterranean Section and initiated the process of (re)publishing these important artifacts.

Bronze Age Figurines from Cyprus

Seven of the figurines described here have been published in *The Coroplastic Art of Ancient Cyprus* series (Karageorghis 1991). The descriptions and discussions, however, were based on the descriptions and photographs published by Max Ohnefalsch-Richter in his *Kypros, the Bible and Homer* (1893). The obvious place to look for these figurines was the Pergamon Museum in Berlin, where most of the Cypriot antiquities excavated by Ohnefalsch-Richter are now housed; thus, it was a pleasant surprise to find them in the University of Pennsylvania Museum in 1994.

Although some of the figurines are published here for the first time, the description and commentary of others have already appeared in print. These latter are presented again here because Dr. Karageorghis has had the opportunity not only to examine them in person, but also after they had been cleaned and properly conserved. The removal of the surface encrustations and dirt has made possible a more accurate identification of their fabrics and forms.

The figurines published here all come from the well-known Bronze Age cemetery of Ayia Paraskevi where Ohnefalsch-Richter excavated a number of tombs in 1884–1885 (Kromholz 1982: 4–5). The necropolis of Ayia Paraskevi is situated on a plateau in the southern part of Nicosia, where the Hilton Hotel now stands. As a pupil at the Nicosia Gymnasium, Dr. Karageorghis often visited the numerous rock-cut chamber tombs of this vast cemetery and collected sherds of Red Polished and White Painted ware from the Early and Middle Bronze Ages. In 1884–1885, Ohnefalsch-Richter excavated eleven tombs for the Cyprus Museum and eighty-one for various residents (Myres and Ohnefalsch-Richter 1899: 1). Myres opened fourteen tombs in 1894 (Myres and Ohnefalsch-Richter 1899: 1) and in later years the Department of Antiquities of Cyprus excavated tombs discovered there accidentally. The British Museum, London, and the Ashmolean Museum, Oxford (Frankel 1983: 116–121), possess a large number of objects from the Ayia Paraskevi necropolis excavated by Myres. Another attempt to publish material from this necropolis was made by Susan Kromholz, who published ten tomb groups that are now in the Cyprus Museum (Kromholz 1982). In 1988, J. B. Hennessy and others published the material from a number of Early Bronze Age I tombs that James Stewart excavated in 1955 (Hennessy et al. 1988: 12–24).

These figurines may date to the Middle Cypriot I period, although they can not be related to the ceramic material with which they were found originally. They are examined here typologically, and an attempt is made to place them in the general framework of the development of the coroplastic art of prehistoric Cyprus.

In an earlier work, the origin and significance of plank-shaped figurines, which range chronologically from the Early Cypriot IIIB to the Middle Cypriot I period were discussed in detail (Karageorghis 1991: 49–52). They may have their origins in large-scale wooden *xoana*, or cultic images that were kept in sanctuaries, and these miniature versions may have been placed in tombs as symbols of rebirth and regeneration. Their flat form and incised decoration may be representative of the characteristics of such wooden prototypes. During the same period, the Cypriot coroplast was making other human and animal figurines in the round that were used mainly to decorate "scenic bowls." These figurines are typologically different from and more "naturalistic" than the plank-shaped figurines because they did not serve the same symbolic purpose and did not derive from the same wooden prototypes.

The plank-shaped figurines are always female; occasionally their sex is indicated specifically. Their jewelry (tiaras or crowns, earrings, and necklaces) support their identification as female even when the breasts are not shown. Although their bodies, incised with geometric motifs, may follow the fashion of Red Polished ware vase decoration of the same period, the idea that the decorations on these figurines represent richly decorated garments should not be dismissed (cf. Karageorghis 1991: 50).

The majority of plank-shaped figurines were found in tombs, but some have been reported from settlements. Frankel and Webb, commenting on the fragmentary anthropomorphic figurines that have been found recently at Marki-Alonia and at Alambra-Mouttes, conclude that "they were used and discarded in settlements as well as tombs. Their battered state and domestic associations at Marki and Alambra further suggest that they were not accorded special status or used in designated ceremonial or ritual areas" (Frankel and Webb 1996: 188). Mogelonsky, who published the terracotta figurines from Alambra, reached similar conclusions, stating that "the fragmentary Alambra figurines, and their most definitely secular findspots at the site, suggest that during this period these objects were used not only for funerary or religious practices, but also in daily life" (Mogelonsky 1996: 200).

The fact remains, however, that most plank-shaped figurines were found in tombs and it is unlikely that they were placed there as toys. We know very little about the role of the figurines found in settlements, since very few of them were found in stratified contexts and our knowledge of sanctuaries, or domestic cult places, is non-existent (Coleman et al. 1996: 329). Merrillees proposed that such figurines had some special connections with Cypriot funerary superstitions (1980: 184), but this hypothesis does not bring us any closer to an understanding of their meaning. If they were placed in tombs, then they had a meaning. This meaning should not be different from that associated with the numerous female figurines placed in tombs during the Late Bronze Age. The connection between these figurines and the idea of fertility is strong and any attempt to minimize their symbolism seems unwise. It is true that evidence for Cypriot cult places, whether sanctuaries or domestic cult areas, during the Early and Middle Bronze Ages is unsatisfactory at present. However, now that settlements from this period are being excavated, this lacuna may be filled. It will also be useful to pay more attention to the tomb context of such figurines; for example, are they always found in relationship to male skeletons and where exactly in the tombs were they placed?

Further studies will, no doubt, help us to date the figurines more closely. The Alambra material confirms the Early Cypriot IIIB to Middle Cypriot I date that has hitherto been assigned to most of them. The main excavated phase of the site dates roughly to ca. 1900–1800 B.C. (Coleman et al. 1996: 335).

The fact that all the figurines discussed here are from the same site is of particular interest because it helps in the identification of a regional group of terracottas. A comparison with other groups from the island will be useful.

Fifteen years ago Kromholz wrote, "the reputation of Ayia Paraskevi as a Bronze Age site of great importance rests on a few rather poorly published tomb groups excavated in the nineteenth century . . . [and] eight individual objects excavated in the twentieth century" (1982: 9). It is hoped that the addition of these terracotta figurines in the University of Pennsylvania Museum to the literature, in addition to increasing our understanding of these objects, may also encourage the analysis and publication of similar groups that have lain unrecognized or unstudied in storerooms worldwide.

Catalogue

General Discussion

This catalogue is arranged, more or less, in chronological order. Plank-shaped anthropomorphic figurines are discussed first. References to types follow those in the first volume of *The Coroplastic Art of Ancient Cyprus* series (Karageorghis 1991).

Some of the figurines correspond to types already known from tombs at Vounous and Lapithos. The vast majority of the figurines hitherto known from the Early Cypriot III and Middle Cypriot I periods, however, have no provenance. One may suggest that there was a *koine* style during this period, with the coroplasts being unusually inspired by the main centers of production that were situated along the northern coast. During the Middle Cypriot period, a regional school may have developed at Ayia Paraskevi that specialized in White Painted anthropomorphic and zoomorphic figurines (Kromholz 1982: 270–273).

List of Objects

1. Terracotta human figurine fragment

Fabric: Red Polished ware
Dimensions: Preserved height: 12.4 cm; width: 10.5 cm; thickness: 1.5 cm
University of Pennsylvania Museum catalogue number: MS 85
Published in: Ohnefalsch-Richter 1893: 419, pl. LXXXVI.6;
 Karageorghis 1991: 100–101, fig. 97, no. E6

DESCRIPTION

Recently cleaned. Handmade, solid. The fabric is mostly buff, with a thin core of gray. Roughly rectangular, rather wide and thin, this fragment likely comes from the torso of a plank-shaped figurine. It is missing its head and neck, broken off at shoulder height, and lower body. When viewed in section it is slightly concave.

The surface of the front and back is decorated with incised and gouged motifs. Beginning at the shoulders, there are double–incised chevrons filled with short oblique lines, with five gouged dots between each chevron. This decoration is possibly meant to represent the neckline of a garment. There are two concentric inscribed lozenges, one on either side of the midpoint of the "neckline," possibly to indicate breasts. An oblique incised line, possibly representing arms, begins just below each shoulder, passes through the lozenge, and terminates in a group of three large gouges just above the lower band of decoration. Beside each of these long oblique lines and running parallel to them is a shorter oblique line near the edge of the figurine that ends in a comb decoration. At the bottom are three incised linked lozenges, a circle inscribed within each lozenge, surrounded by two rows of opposed triangles filled with horizontal incisions.

On the back of the figure, at the top just below the shoulders, are the remains of three sets of vertical bands filled with oblique strokes, probably meant to represent tresses of hair. Just below the shoulders on both the left and the right side is a short band composed of double horizontal straight lines on the top and bottom with a double zigzag within. On the same line as these bands, but further in toward the middle of the back, are two sets of short oblique lines arranged vertically. Below each of the top bands on either side is another band composed of short oblique lines arranged horizontally and bordered by a horizontal line. Another two sets of short oblique lines arranged vertically occur between these two bands. This last band of incised decoration with its accompanying two sets of vertical oblique strokes occurs once more below. At the bottom are two incised circles with a row of concentric lozenges above. An incised straight horizontal line runs through the center of all the lozenges. Above the lozenges is a double straight horizontal line.

DISCUSSION

This fragmentary figurine corresponds to types Ba and Bc, shoulder figurines without arms. These types have rectangular bodies and short angular shoulders. The upper part of MS 85 is missing, so it is not certain whether it had ears and thus conformed more to type Ba (without ears) or Bc (with perforated ears).

The use of gouges in association with the incised necklaces and at the terminals of the incised arms is found among other figurines of these types (cf., e.g., Karageorghis 1991: 52, 57, 63–65, pls. XX.1, XXIII.3, XXIX.3, XXX.1,2, XXXI.1, nos. Ba.1, 12, Bc.13, 15, 16, 20). The rich decoration on the body, on both front and back, may be compared with other plank-shaped figurines (cf. Karageorghis 1991: 52–53, 56, 63–64, pls. XX.1, 2, 3, XXI.2, XXII.1, XXX.1,2, nos. Ba.1, 2, 3, 8, 9, Bc.15, 16).

1a. Red Polished ware human figurine fragment. Front view. (1:1).

1b. Red Polished ware human figurine fragment. Rear view. (1:1).

2. Terracotta human female figurine

Fabric: Red Polished ware
Dimensions: Preserved height: 13.0 cm; width (at right arm): 8.7 cm;
    thickness (not including right breast): 1.5 cm
University of Pennsylvania Museum catalogue number: MS 78
Published in: Ohnefalsch-Richter 1893: 419, pl. LXXXVI.5;
    Karageorghis 1991: 77, fig. 79, no. Bg.8

DESCRIPTION

Handmade, solid. The fabric is orange-buff in color, light gray at the core. The polished surface is dark red to nearly black in some places. This flat, roughly rectangular figure is partially preserved: the lower body has broken off and both the left arm and left breast are missing. In addition, the head has been damaged by chipping. It is slightly concave in section. The head is indicated only by a slightly rounded top. No facial features are shown. The neck is elongated and very wide, being the same width as the head. The right breast is shown in relief. Judging from the appearance of the right breast and from the traces remaining of the left breast, it seems that the breasts were created by applying a rolled ball of clay to the figurine and then smoothing down the clay to blend with the rest of the body. The right arm projects from the torso and curves downward; neither hands nor fingers are depicted. The right arm and shoulder area are decorated on the front and the back with groups of incised dotted lines. Traces of such lines indicate that the left arm and shoulder were treated in a similar fashion, possibly to indicate clothing. The upper parts of the body and head are decorated with three incised horizontal bands filled with oblique lines. An incised zigzag line runs horizontally across the object below the upper two horizontal bands. Similar horizontal bands decorate the lower portion of the figurine: one band appears just above the breasts and between the arms, while two more run across the front of the object and traces of a third appear at the bottom. Above this third partial band there is a second horizontal zigzag line. The back of the figurine is also decorated with incised lines. There are vertical incised zigzags along the head and neck, possibly to represent tresses of hair. Below these, almost in the middle of the back, are two opposed sets of two parallel vertical dotted lines running part of the way down the back. Numerous dotted horizontal lines run out to the side of the figurine all along the length of the parallel vertical lines. Below the arms on each side is a single vertical zigzag. Traces of white filling, possibly lime, remain in some of the incised decoration, particularly on the back of the figurine.

DISCUSSION

This piece is type Bg, a shoulder figurine with stubby arms. The right arm is complete as it is preserved, in contrast to what was implied in the previously published drawing (Karageorghis 1991: 77, fig. 79, no. Bg.8). The breasts are shown. No doubt due to imperfect firing, the color of the surface varies from orange-buff to nearly black. The dotted horizontal lines on the shoulders, on both front and back, suggest a shoulder wrap, as is found on other similar figurines (Karageorghis 1991: 82, 85–86, pls. XLIX.3, L.1, nos. Bi.4 [no. MS 75 below], Bj.4, 6). Morris suggested that

2a. Red Polished ware human female figurine. Front view. (1:1)

this may be a "shoulder-cape" (1985: 146). It is possible that this "cape" formed part of a garment worn by special people on special occasions (cf. Karageorghis 1991: 10, with regard to Cypriot figurines of the Chalcolithic period).

2b. Red Polished ware human female figurine. Rear view. (1:1)

3. Terracotta human female figurine

Fabric: Red Polished ware
Dimensions: Preserved height: 13.7 cm; width (at elbows): 6.4 cm;
      thickness (not including arms): 1.5 cm
University of Pennsylvania Museum catalogue number: MS 77
Published in: Ohnefalsch-Richter 1893: 419, pl. LXXXVI.4;
      Karageorghis 1991: 88, fig. 90, no. Bj.17

DESCRIPTION

Recently cleaned. Handmade, solid. The fabric is orange-buff in color, dark gray at the core. The polished is light red to nearly brown in some places. On the reverse, the surface is blackened slightly in an area on the left side. This flat, rectangular, rounded figurine is in a good state of preservation with the exception of the head, which has been broken diagonally across the top. Thus, the top of the head, the left side of the face, and the left ear are missing. The surface has been chipped in several places and the polish is generally abraded. The figurine is slightly concave in section. The right eye is indicated by a small, diagonal depression. The mouth is rendered by a similar depression, gouged upward at a sharp angle. Traces remain of a pinched nose. The projecting right ear flares out from the head and curves in toward the face in a concave fashion. It is pierced in three places along the edge. The very broad and elongated neck widens from the head toward the sloping shoulders of the figurine and is ornamented near the face by an applied ridge that is decorated with diagonal, horizontal, and vertically incised grooves. The breasts are depicted at shoulder height, shown in relief and with a depression in the center to indicate the nipples. Short applied arms are also shown in relief held out in front of and touching the body directly below the breasts. Each hand ends in three fingers represented by long incised grooves. There is a deep vertically incised groove gouged upward at a sharp angle near the bottom of the figurine indicating the genitals. Besides this incision, the lower half of the front of the figurine is roughly portrayed, the details of the lower body and even the legs omitted. The reverse side is decorated with two sets of incised lines. At the top, on the back of the head, there are four vertically incised zigzag lines to represent hair. At the bottom, at the same height as the depicted genitalia on the front, there are two horizontal bands of incised decoration filled with short diagonal and horizontal incisions.

DISCUSSION

This piece is type Bj, a slab figurine without legs, but with large, perforated ears and arms marked in relief; incisions indicate fingers. The breasts are clearly shown in relief, with a slit for each nipple. This feature, together with the indication of the genitalia with an incision and the presence of large perforated ears, is characteristic of the developed plank-shaped figurine types such as Bi and Bj (Karageorghis 1991: 82–84, 87–89, pls. XLVIII.4, 5, LI.1, 6, 8, nos. Bi.4, 5, 9, Bj.12, 18, 21). Typologically this figurine has many parallels in types Bi and Bj (Karageorghis 1991: 81–89, pls. XLVIII–LI).

3a. Red Polished ware human female figurine. Front view. (1:1).

3b. Red Polished ware human female figurine. Rear view. (1:1).

4. Terracotta human female figurine

Fabric: Red Polished ware

Dimensions: Preserved height: 14.3 cm; width (at elbows): 8.0 cm;
thickness (at right arm): 2.4 cm

University of Pennsylvania Museum catalogue number: MS 75

Published in: Ohnefalsch-Richter 1893: 33, 420, fig. 30, pl. LXXXVI.7;
Karageorghis 1991: 82, no. Bi.4

Description

Handmade, solid. The fabric is buff in color, gray at the core. This flat, thin
female figure is mostly preserved except for the lower part of the body,
which is broken off above the waist. It is concave in section. Above the wide,
highly elongated neck is a rectangular head, with features variously formed:
gouged round eyes, incised mouth, prominent nose in relief with incised
nostrils. At the top of the head there is a horizontal ridge with oblique incisions, possibly to indicate hair or a veil or other head-covering. These incisions are filled with a white substance. In addition, strips of clay were applied
to the back and sides of the head to depict wavy locks of hair. Clay strips were
also applied to the neck as a necklace: one wavy strand between two horizontal strands. The bottom horizontal strand continues around the back of
the figurine. Breasts, shown in relief, seem to have been formed by pinching
up the clay and gouging holes for nipples. Starting at each breast is a vertical incised line that travels down the figurine between the arms ending in a
gouged hole. The arms are shown in relief, held in front of the figure touching the body and with fingers incised. On the figurine's right side, both front
and back, there are incised dimples on the lower part of the neck, shoulder,
and arm, possibly to indicate a garment. Just below the sloping shoulders are
two parallel incised lines running horizontally across the front of the figure,
which are decorated with a single row of incised dimples, possibly to indicate
the top of the dress.

Discussion

This figurine resembles those of type Bj, the depressions for the eyes and slit
for the mouth and nostrils being comparable (e.g., Karageorghis 1991: 85–86,
fig. 88, pl. XLIX.4, no. Bj.5). The vertical wavy bands in relief for the hair on
the back of the head are, however, a unique feature; the locks of hair on other
figurines of this type are usually indicated with incised wavy lines (e.g., Karageorghis 1991: 85–86, figs. 87, 88, pls. XLIX.3, 4, L.2, nos. Bj.4, 5, 7). The
same may be said about the triple necklace in relief composed of two straight
and one wavy band across the neck. The figurine wears a "shoulder-cape" similar to that of MS 78. Although the arms are rendered in relief, with the fingers shown with incisions, the coroplast indicates a second pair of arms, with
almost vertical incised lines terminating in a gouge. These secondary arms are
obviously an element from the past that the coroplast did not understand.
The same phenomenon appears on other figurines of the same type (e.g.,
Karageorghis 1991: 81–82, fig. 82, pl. XLVIII.1, no. Bi.1, and cf. 93).

4a. Red Polished ware human female figurine. Front View. (1:1).

4b. Red Polished ware human female figurine. Rear View. (1:1).

5. Terracotta human female figurine

Fabric: Red Polished ware
Dimensions: Preserved height: 14.8 cm; preserved width (at ears): 5.6 cm;
     thickness (not including breasts): 2.0 cm
University of Pennsylvania Museum catalogue number: MS 79
Published in: Ohnefalsch-Richter 1893: 108–109, 192, 419, pl. LXXXVI.2;
     Karageorghis 1991: 88–89, fig. 91, no. Bj.20

DESCRIPTION

Handmade, solid. The fabric is buff, gray at the core. This flat, roughly rectangular figure is rounded at the top and roughly flat at the bottom, no legs
being depicted. The surface is very worn, pitted, and chipped. The lower portion of the figure is broken off and both ears are chipped. It is likely that the
figure had arms at one time, but these are now broken off. The elongated
neck and head of the figure are indicated by a slight narrowing and rounding at one end. The face is conveyed by a simple depression possibly made by
pressing a finger into the clay. There are no facial characteristics depicted.
On either side of and below this depression are short incised lines radiating
outward. Projecting on either side of the head are the remains of large
applied ears, which appear to have been double-pierced at one time. Below
the right ear is a circular decoration in relief possibly representing a loop ear-
ring. It seems likely that a similar decoration was present below the left ear,
though this area is damaged now, making it difficult to tell with any certainty.
The top of the head above the face is decorated with a wide horizontal
incised zigzag with two horizontal incised lines below. Horizontal incised
lines and dotted lines decorate the neck area. Well below the facial area are
two raised lumps, probably breasts depicted in relief. Just below these pro-
jections, on both right and left sides, the figure is damaged. Judging from the
remains it seems that applied features were attached here, probably arms,
and that they subsequently broke off. Between the remains of the two arms
there are incised horizontal zigzag and dotted lines. The body of the figure
below the arms is decorated with alternating horizontal incised straight lines
and zigzags. On the back of the figurine, starting from the top of the head
and extending down several centimeters, are incised vertical zigzag lines representing tresses. Just below these zigzags is a shallow abraded groove, about
3 cm in height, running horizontally from one side of the figurine to the
other where the surface has been scraped away and the fabric is visible.

DISCUSSION

This piece belongs to type Bj. It has a peculiar rendering of the face with an
ovoid cavity with radiating strokes all around it. Ohnefalsch-Richter called it
a "radiant or sun-face" (1893: 419). The hollow can not have had a nose that
later became detached because, like the rest of the face, it is covered with a
slip. This is not one of the most carefully rendered figurines of this type. The
neck is fused to the shoulders without any separation and the arms are not
shown. The engraved decoration is rather carelessly rendered.

5a. Red Polished ware human female figurine. Front view. (1:1).

5b. Red Polished ware human female figurine. Rear view. (1:1).

6. Terracotta human figurine
Fabric: White Painted ware
University of Pennsylvania Museum catalogue number: MS 80
Dimensions: Preserved height: 7.1 cm; width (across elbows): 4.9 cm;
      thickness: 2.1 cm

DECRIPTION
Handmade, solid. The fabric is buff, light gray at the core. The figurine is
rather worn and dirty. Only the torso, arms, and lower body are preserved
from this narrow figurine, the head, neck, and legs (if depicted) having
been lost. It is oval when viewed in section. The arms are depicted in
relief, separate pieces of clay being applied to the torso, and are shown as
being held around in front and touching the body. The hands end in
incised fingers. The decoration consists of geometric patterns painted in
a dark reddish-brown shiny paint. In general, the state of the surface of
the figurine makes it too difficult to discern the decorative motifs.
Although much of the paint has flaked away, it does appear that there are
several sets of straight horizontal lines and zigzags painted on the back of
the figurine.

6. White Painted Ware human figurine. *Left:* Front view. (1:1). *Right:* Rear
view (1:1).

Discussion

This piece is published here for the first time. It is of White Painted ware and may be compared typologically to the Red Polished equivalent, namely type Bj, with arms in relief and fingers indicated with grooves (Karageorghis 1991: 84–89, pls. XLIX–LI). There is another plank-shaped figurine of White Painted ware from Ayia Paraskevi (Karageorghis 1991: 171, pl. CXXXVI.5, no. WHP.Bj.3), now in the Cyprus Museum, Nicosia.

7. Terracotta human female figurine

Fabric: Red Polished ware
Dimensions: Preserved height: 4.8 cm; preserved width (at arms): 2.5 cm;
    thickness (including breasts): 0.9 cm
University of Pennsylvania Museum catalogue number: MS 81
Published in: Ohnefalsch-Richter 1893: 419, pl. LXXXVI.1;
    Karageorghis 1991: 138, no. V.5

Handmade, solid. The fabric is buff, gray at the core. Small, flat, roughly rectangular and rounded at one end, this object is probably an anthropomorphic plank-shaped figurine that was once attached to a vase. It is extremely worn, is missing its left arm, broken off at the shoulder, and is chipped at the bottom. The head and neck are indicated by the rounding and slight narrowing of one end. No facial characteristics are indicated. The right arm projects out and down from the body, but there are no indications of a hand or fingers. Two raised lumps, breasts depicted in relief, are located below the facial region of the figure and between the arms.

7. Red Polished Ware human figurine. *Left:* Front view (2:1). *Right:* Rear view (2:1).

8. Terracotta cradle figurine

Fabric: White Painted ware
Dimensions: Preserved height: 13.1 cm; width: 5.8 cm; thickness: 2.3 cm
University of Pennsylvania Museum catalogue number: MS 76
Published in: Ohnefalsch-Richter 1893: 419, pl. LXXXVI.3;
　　　　　Karageorghis 1991: 95, fig. 93, no. C5

DESCRIPTION
Recently cleaned. Handmade, solid. The fabric is buff, gray at the core. This cradle figurine is very worn and only partially preserved, being chipped and abraded at the top and missing the lower part of the cradle. It is oval in section. The stylized figure of the child is depicted in relief against the flat surface of the cradle. At the top, the object bulges out slightly on each side to form the base of the protective arch. All that remains of this arch, however, is the abraded base of its left side. Below the bulge the figurine narrows and forms the background for the representation of the infant: an elongated, narrowing neck ending in a pointed head with prominent nose and shallow depressions for eyes. Above each of the infant's shoulders, near the base of the neck, is a breast in relief. Two short arms, the left one only partially preserved, bend around to hold the infant at its shoulders. Below the shoulders the figurine continues without any further depiction of the shape of the infant, presumably because it was obscured by some type of covering. The figurine is decorated with matte dark brownish-red paint: the upper part of the cradle and infant have alternating painted horizontal straight and zigzag lines and the area of the infant represented as bundled has a painted lattice pattern. Below this pattern, there are traces of another horizontal zigzag. The back is plain except for numerous painted vertical zigzag lines at the top meant to represent tresses.

DISCUSSION
When this figurine was described as Red Polished ware (Karageorghis 1991: 95, fig. 93, no. C5), the assessment was based on the photograph published by Ohnefalsch-Richter (1893: 419, pl. LXXXVI.3). After cleaning, the piece has proven to be of White Painted ware. Merrillees believed the figurine to be a hermaphrodite with an erect phallus held between its hands (1980: 174). The figure is, rather, holding a cradle figurine similar to another where one may see clearly the protective curved arch of the cradle preserved above the face of the stylized infant (cf. Karageorghis 1991: 95, pl. LII.4, no. C4). On MS 76 the arch was broken off, but the breaks are still visible (cf. Karageorghis 1991: 97). On the back of the cradle the hair of a female figure is indicated with vertical zigzag lines. This feature is also found on the example cited above (Karageorghis 1991: no. C4; cf. 97). This hair suggests a "personification" of the cradle, or rather a confusion of the cradle figurine with a female shoulder figurine. It is not impossible that this may be an intentional fusion of the figurine of a mother with that of an infant in a cradle (cf. also Karageorghis 1991: 96, pl. LII.5, no. C6, where the cradle is also "personified" with a female figure fused with two infants, each in a separate cradle).

8a. White Painted ware cradle figurine. Front view. (1:1)

8b. White Painted ware cradle figurine. Rear view. (1:1)

9. Terracotta human figurine fragment

Fabric: White Painted ware

Dimensions: Preserved height: 7.8 cm; preserved width (at top): 2.8 cm;
    preserved thickness: 0.9 cm

University of Pennsylvania Museum catalogue number: MS 84

DESCRIPTION

Handmade, solid. The fabric is a buff clay, fired buff all the way through, with a white slip. This fragment consists of the lower legs and feet of a figurine, broken off at or slightly below the knees. The legs seem to have been fashioned separately from cylinders of clay, then pressed together and joined at the bottom to form a single "foot." The toes are not indicated. Each leg is decorated similarly with bands of matte dark reddish-brown paint: three horizontal bands at the top near the knees, two wavy bands in the middle of the legs, then four horizontal bands above the ankles. The groove where the two cylinders of clay were joined to make the legs is also painted, both front and back, with the same type of paint.

DISCUSSION

This fragmentary White Painted ware figurine is published here for the first time. Typologically it corresponds to figurines with long legs (e.g., White

9. White Painted ware human figurine fragment. *Left:* Front view. (1:1). *Right:* Rear view (1:1).

Painted ware figurines in Karageorghis 1991: 179, fig. 138, pl. CXLI.1, nos. WHP.Eb.1, 2; and a Red Slip figurine in the Musée des Beaux-Arts in Lyon in Decaudin 1987: 109–110, pl. XLIV.57, no. 57). The closest parallel, however, is a White Painted ware nude female figurine now in the Pitt Rivers Collection in Oxford that will be published at a later date (inv. no. 1921.54.1).

10. Terracotta figurine of a bovine (?) quadruped
Fabric: Red Polished ware
Dimensions: Preserved height (at lug): 5.7 cm; preserved length: 6.9 cm; width (at feet): 2.5 cm
University of Pennsylvania Museum catalogue number: MS 72

DESCRIPTION
Handmade, solid. The fabric is light brown in color. The piece is rather worn and somewhat chipped. The block-like body of this free-standing quadruped roughly conveys the shape of a bovine creature with short, stubby, and rounded legs, thick neck, and traces of a pinched tail. Three of the feet, made by pinching down the clay from the central mass of the object, are roughly intact while the front right foot is missing. The head has broken off at the base of the neck. In the middle of the top of the object (the back of the quadruped) is an arched lug pierced by a hole, possibly for suspension. The object is decorated with patterns of incisions. The sides are decorated similarly: a vertical band delineated by solid incised lines and filled with short oblique strokes appears in the middle of each side and runs from the top near the lug to the bottom. Flanking this vertical band on the left and the right are three horizontal bands also delineated by solid incised lines and filled with short oblique strokes. The top is decorated with similar bands of incisions: one transverse band filled with incised oblique strokes is on either side of the pierced lug. On the front of the figurine, at the base of the neck, there is another incised band, also filled with short oblique strokes. The rear of the figurine is decorated more simply: a simple incised vertical straight line with a gouged hole at either end.

DISCUSSION
This piece is published here for the first time. It is a figurine of a quadruped, corresponding to type G (e.g., Karageorghis 1991: 103, pl. LVIII.4, no. G.13; cf. also Frankel and Webb 1996: 188–189, fig. 8.4, pl. 33g, no. P2371). The neck and the tail are missing. There are several zoomorphic askoi from this period, but solid free-standing terracotta quadruped figurines are rare (Frankel and Webb 1996: 188–189; Mogelonsky 1996: 203–204). They are more common as accessories decorating the rim or shoulder of vases (e.g., Karageorghis 1991: 120–122, pls. LXXX.1, 2, LXXXIV.9, 10, 11, nos. SC9, SC14a7, 8, 9).

10. Red Polished ware figurine of a bovine (?) quadruped. (1:1).

11. Terracotta figurine of a bovine (?) quadruped

Fabric: Red Polished ware
Dimensions: Preserved height: 4.6 cm; preserved length: 6.4 cm;
      width: 1.9 cm
University of Pennsylvania Museum catalogue number: MS 71

DESCRIPTION

Handmade, solid. The fabric is orange-buff in color. The angular, block-like body of this freestanding quadruped is supported by short, stubby legs and has a knobby tail. The head is missing, broken off at the base of the neck, as are both the right front and rear legs. The body is very narrow in width in proportion to its length. Along the back of the quadruped there is a spine-like ridge, made by pinching up the clay, with two shallow troughs beside this ridge running parallel to it. In the middle of the back on either side there are three evenly spaced parallel incised notches near the edge.

DISCUSSION

This piece is another free-standing quadruped figurine that is published here for the first time (cf. Karageorghis 1991: 103–104, pl. LVIII.5, no. G.14). The two shallow troughs on either side of the spine may represent panniers on the animal's back. A comparable piece, no. G.14, cited above, is now exhibited in the Semitic Museum at Harvard University where it was to re-examined by the author in April 1997. It has a flat base that was created in recent times by sawing away the stub legs of the figure so that the piece can stand freely.

11. Red Polished ware figurine of a bovine (?) quadruped. *Left:* End view (1:1). *Right:* Side view (1:1).

12. Terracotta figurine of a deer (?)
Fabric: Red Polished ware
Dimensions: Height: 4.3 cm; length: 6.4 cm; preserved width
      (at antlers): 4.1 cm
University of Pennsylvania Museum catalogue number: MS 69

DESCRIPTION
Handmade, solid. The fabric is a fine, buff clay with few inclusions. Though very worn, there are still traces of thick red polished slip on the surface of the object. The body of this quadruped is amorphous, block-like and roughly conveyed, with only the head and face receiving detailed treatment by the coroplast. The head is large and is topped by branching, many-pointed horns. The left horn is broken off and the right is chipped. Below the horns, ears are depicted in relief; the right ear is intact but the left is only partially preserved. The eyes are conveyed by two deeply gouged holes; the mouth and nostrils are incised on the protruding snout. The haunches and legs of the animal are indicated only by a slight rise in the otherwise shapeless body. A slight bump on the rump of the figurine may represent a tail, though this spot is very worn. The base of the figurine spreads out in a bell-like fashion and is slightly concave and unfinished.

DISCUSSION
This piece was obviously detached from the rim or the shoulder of a vase, like many examples known from the site of Vounous (e.g., Karageorghis 1991: 147–148, pls. CVI.3, CX.1, 2, nos. VIII.4, IX.5, 6).

12. Red Polished ware figurine of a deer (?). (1:1).

13. Terracotta figurine of a bull's head, detached from a vessel
Fabric: Red Polished ware
Dimensions: Height (at back): 3.9 cm; width (at greatest point between horns): 4.0 cm
University of Pennsylvania Museum catalogue number: MS 70

DESCRIPTION
Handmade, solid. The fabric is brownish-buff in color. This roughly made bull's head has rounded horns projecting forward and upward at an angle. The figurine's right horn was broken but is now mended. The eyes are indicated by large, deeply gouged holes; the mouth is rendered by a simple incised straight line. Ears are depicted in relief against the base of the horn, with the left ear being less worn and thus more clearly distinguishable. The underside of the object is unfinished and slightly concave. Like MS 69, discussed above, this piece was detached from the wall of a vase (cf., e.g., Karageorghis 1991: 155, pl. CXX.1, no. XI.25).

13. Red Polished ware figurine of a bulls head. (2:1).

14. Terracotta figurine of a bird

Fabric: Red Polished ware
Dimensions: Preserved height (from pedestal to top of neck): 4.3 cm;
        preserved length: 6.3 cm; width: 2.4 cm
University of Pennsylvania Museum catalogue number: MS 73

DESCRIPTION

Handmade, solid. The fabric is medium red in color, orange at the core. The piece is rather worn and much covered in concretions. This figurine depicts a long-necked bird with almond-shaped body perching with its wings folded. It is mostly intact, except for the head, which is broken off at the end of the neck. Instead of feet the figurine has the remains of a clay pedestal that may have served as an attachment point to another vessel. The folded wings are indicated by three incised furrows on the back with feathers depicted by a herringbone pattern of incisions. The majority of these wing incisions are filled with a white material that could possibly be lime or paint, or perhaps concretions.

DISCUSSION

This figure was also detached from the wall of a vase (cf., e.g., Karageorghis 1991: 155, 158–159, pls. CXX.2, CXXIII–CXXVI, nos. XI.26, XII.2–14). This style of decoration was particularly favored by the potters of Vounous (cf. Karageorghis 1991: 162–163).

14. Red Polished ware figurine of a bird. (1:1).

15. Terracotta model of a table (fragment)

Fabric: Red Polished ware
Dimensions: Height: 14.0 cm; width: 9.5 cm; thickness (excluding
    projection): 1.5 cm
University of Pennsylvania Museum catalogue number: MS 488
Published in: Ohnefalsch-Richter 1893: 372, pl. XXXVI.9

DESCRIPTION
Handmade, solid. The fabric is buff in color, dark gray at the core. Mended
from two pieces, this object is probably a fragment from a model of a table.
Plank-like and rather thin, it narrows at one end and is broken across the
middle. Near the narrow end is a knob-like broken projection, possibly the
remains of the stem of a bowl. It is decorated with various incised motifs.
At the wide end of the upper side there are five roughly straight horizontal incised lines running the width of the piece. Beside these are two concentric circles, one on either side. Another set of five horizontal lines lies
beyond the circles, adjacent to the projection. On either side of the projection is a concentric circle, and beyond each of these is a row of short vertical strokes running along the of the object. The end is decorated with
groups of horizontal straight lines running from side to side, the full width
of the object: six lines at the narrower end, four lines in the middle, and
five lines at the wider end.

DISCUSSION
This piece is a fragment from a model of a table, on the flat top of which
bowls were attached. Only one fragmentary bowl is preserved on MS 488.
There was a second fragment that belonged to the same table. It is illustrated by Ohnefalsch-Richter (1893: 372, pl. XXXVI.2), but its where-
abouts are unknown. Models of tables with bowls on their flat tops are
known in the coroplastic art of this period from tombs at Vounous and
Lapithos (cf. Karageorghis 1991: 106, pls. LIX.1, 2, nos. Ha.1, 2, also 1991,
108 for discussion).

15a. Red Polished ware model of a table fragment. Upperside. (1:1).

15b. Red Polished ware model of a table fragment. Underside. (1:1).

16. Terracotta model of a horn
Fabric: Red Polished ware
Dimensions: Height: 9.8 cm; diameter: 3.2 cm
University of Pennsylvania Museum catalogue number: MS 74

DESCRIPTION
Handmade, hollow. The fabric is buff in color. The object is very worn and somewhat abraded. This conical vessel tapers to a point and then curves out to the side near its closed end, conveying the image of a horn. It is circular in section and rather worn. The open end has an in-curving rim, about one-half of which is missing. Just below the rim, the wall of the vessel is pierced by a small round hole, possibly for suspension. The interior has been smoothed clean along most of its length except for a spot halfway down the inside where it appears that there was once a thin layer of clay separating the top half from the bottom half. Subsequently this layer was pierced with a narrow implement, joining the two halves but leaving a thin ledge of clay on the interior. These traces may indicate that the object was made in two separate pieces that were joined together and the excess bonding clay reamed out with a stick. The body of the vessel is decorated with short horizontal incisions grouped in threes and arranged in a checkerboard fashion all around the outside. The interior is plain.

DISCUSSION
This piece is a horn model, a type that was quite popular as a tomb gift at Vounous (e.g., Karageorghis 1991: 114–116, pls. LXIII.–LXIV, type Hd).

16. Red Polished ware model of a horn. (1:1).

17. Terracotta model of a spoon or ladle

Fabric: Monochrome ware
Dimensions: Length: 5.8 cm; diameter (of bowl): 2.2 cm;
          diameter (of handle): 1.2 cm
University of Pennsylvania Museum catalogue number: MS 91

DESCRIPTION
Handmade, solid. The fabric appears to be buff. The surface is mostly covered with a white substance, possibly a slip or concretion. In several places there seem to be the remains of a greenish-brown paint. The spoon or ladle is mostly intact, except for certain small chips, and slightly worn. The rolled cylindrical stem, round in section, ends in a small hemispherical bowl. Apart from the possible paint, the object is undecorated.

DISCUSSION
This spoon measures 5.8 cm in length. Catling suggested that such terracotta spoons were actually used for eating (1993: 131), but it is rather doubtful when we consider how easily one could make a wooden spoon as is done today. Wooden spoons are lighter and more durable.

17. Plainware model of a spoon or ladle. (2:1).

Bibliography

Buchholz, H. G.
1989 Max Ohnefalsch-Richter als Archäologe auf Zypern. *Centre d'*
Études Chypriotes, cahier 11-12: 3–27 (with further bibliography).

Catling, H. W.
1993 Vassos Karageorghis: *The Coroplastic Art of Ancient Cyprus, Vol. I:*
Chalcolithic-Late Cypriote I (review article). *The Classical Review* 43:
129–131.

Coleman, J. E. et al.
1996 *Alambra, A Middle Bronze Age Settlement in Cyprus: Archaeological*
Investigations by Cornell University 1974–1985 (*Studies in Mediter-*
ranean Archaeology CXVIII). Jonsered.

Decaudin, A. J.
1987 *Les antiquités chypriotes dans les collections publiques françaises*. Nicosia.

Fivel, L.
1989 Ohnefalsch-Richter (1850–1917), essai de bibliographie. *Centre*
d'Études Chypriotes, cahier 11-12: 35–40.

Frankel, D.
1983 *Corpus of Cypriote Antiquities 7. Early and Middle Bronze Age Material*
in the Ashmolean Museum, Oxford (*Studies in Mediterranean Archaeol-*
ogy XX:7). Göteborg.

Frankel, D. and J. M. Webb
1996 *Marki Alonia, An Early and Middle Bronze Age Town in Cyprus: Exca-*
vations 1990–1994 (*Studies in Mediterranean Archaeology* CXXIII.1).
Jonsered.

Hennessy, J. B., K. O. Eriksson, and I. C. Kehrberg
1988 *Ayia Paraskevi and Vasilia. Excavations by J. R. B. Stewart* (*Studies in*
Mediterranean Archaeology LXXXII). Göteborg.

Hermary, A.
1990 Ohnefalsch-Richter à Amathonte. *Centre d'Études Chypriotes, cahier*
13: 21–26.

Karageorghis, V.
1991 *The Coroplastic Art of Ancient Cyprus I. Chalcolithic-Late Cypriote I.*
      Nicosia.

Kromholz, S. F.
1982 *The Bronze Age Necropolis at Ayia Paraskevi (Nicosia): Unpublished
      Tombs in the Cyprus Museum* (*Studies in Mediterranean Archaeology
      Pocket-book* 17). Göteborg.

Marangou, A. G. and A. Malecos (eds.)
n.d. *Studies in Cyprus* (Cultural Center Cyprus Popular Bank edition of
      original 1895 album by M. Ohnefalsch-Richter and M. Ohne-
      falsch-Richter). Nicosia.

Masson, O.
1985 Les visites de Max Ohnefalsch-Richter à Kouklia (ancienne
      Paphos), 1890 et 1910. *Centre d'Études Chypriotes, cahier 3:* 19–28.

1986 Illustrations complémentaires pour le voyage de Max Ohnefalsch-
      Richter à Kouklia en 1890. *Centre d'Études Chypriotes, cahier 5:* 33.

Masson, O. and A. Hermary
1988 Les fouilles d'Ohnefalsch-Richter à Idalion en 1894. *Centre d'É-
      tudes Chypriotes, cahier 10* (1988-2): 3–14.

Merrillees, R. S.
1980 Representation of the Human Form in Prehistoric Cyprus. *Opus-
      cula Atheniensia* XIII: 171–184.

Mogelonsky, M. K.
1996 V.E. Moveable Finds: Terracotta. In Coleman, J. E., et al., *Alambra,
      A Middle Bronze Age Settlement in Cyprus: Archaeological Investigations
      by Cornell University 1974–1985*, pp. 199–236. (*Studies in Mediter-
      ranean Archaeology* CXVIII). Jonsered.

Morris, D.
1985 *The Art of Ancient Cyprus.* Oxford.

Myres, J. L. and M. Ohnefalsch-Richter
1899 *A Catalogue of the Cyprus Museum.* Oxford.

Ohnefalsch-Richter, M.
1893 *Kypros, the Bible and Homer.* London (also in German).